The Infinite Doctrine of Water

Also by Michael T. Young

The Beautiful Moment of Being Lost
Transcriptions of Daylight
Living in the Counterpoint (chapbook)
Because the Wind Has Questions (chapbook)

The Infinite Doctrine
of
Water

Michael T. Young

Terrapin Books

© 2018 by Michael T. Young
Printed in the United States of America
All rights reserved.
No part of this book may be reproduced in any manner, except for brief quotations embodied in critical articles or reviews.

Terrapin Books
4 Midvale Avenue
West Caldwell, NJ 07006

www.terrapinbooks.com

ISBN: 978-1-947896-01-7
LCCN: 2018932877

First Edition

Cover art: *Waterfall,* by Eva Schmidseder

for Chandra, Ariel, and Malia

Contents

I
Advice from a Bat	7
Contrast	8
Molting	9
Birdwatcher	10
Learning How to Hunger	11
Feeding the Chameleon	12
The Reservoir	13
The Infinite Doctrine of Water	14
Bioluminescence	15
Turpentine	16

II
New Pens	19
Cipher	20
Study for Infatuation	21
Learning to Read the Ice	22
Spy Game	23
Reading for Pleasure	24
Sage	25
Surfacing	26
Scraps	27
The Generosity of the Past	28
Setting Fires	30
Counting Apples	31

III
Treading Water	35
Renewing My Passport	36
Close Reading	37
Chain Links	38
Fire Eater	39
How a Bridge Is Built	40
Collecting Coins	41
Counting Change	42
Private Constellations	43
The Longest Hibernation	44
Devotional	45

IV

Breadcrumbs	49
How We Learn	50
Some Cracks	51
What It Was Like	52
After Rain	53
Tuning In	54
A Remaining Shot	55
Below Deck	56
My Jersey City	57
Seed	58
Chestnut	59

V

Like Rain	63
Following the Clues	64
Tailor-made	65
Paperclip	66
Bless the Scavengers	67
Signature	68
Peculiar Smoke	69
The Voice of Water	70

Acknowledgments	73
About the Author	77

*What is the past if not unfinished work,
swampy, fecund, seductively revisable?*
—Stephen Dunn

I

Advice from a Bat

Hunt only at night. Fly erratically.
Defy even your own expectations.
Feed on beetles, moths, and mosquitoes,
whatever is small and annoying.
Cultivate the myths about you
until every predator fears your legend.
When hunting, be guided by a language
only you can hear. The same is true
when courting the one you love.
Clean fangs and fur nightly. Crawl
or climb to confuse the observant.
Retreat to a cave no one believes in.
Let the day and the world pass
while you sleep, and sleep upside down,
ready to wake and fall into flight.

Contrast

The early instant cameras were not so instant.
There was a precise count before pulling
the sleeve from the camera, before tugging
the tabs loose and seeing the image surface
as out of mist, so I never felt sure
it was finished, that it might get clearer
if I kept waiting, that more might come back
in time, the way we waited for Dad in the car
because he was always last out of the house,
making sure the doors and windows were locked.

It was 1974 during the gas crisis and once a week
we waited in a car line that was blocks long to fill
a brown Plymouth Scamp with tan vinyl interior,
a hideous machine the same color as the rock face
around the bend from the gas station, a sheer
jagged rise topped by scots pine and sugar maple,
in turn topped by circling robins and cirrus clouds
that mesmerized me by seeming to thin without
fading, until their slight bodies were so strained,
their white only seemed to deepen the sky's blue.

Molting

She browses bird books and whistles
to herself. At night, to lift her dreams

from the mundane, she nests in
a cradle of down pillows. In the morning,

she lights a candle, dips her finger
in a puddle of wax, lets it cool on the tip

to remember the flight of Daedalus,
who, unlike his son, winged coolly on.

She collects feathers in a book and flips
the pages over to feel the air, forgetting

what holds her down or back, everyone
who told her she'd never take flight, ride

desire to the far mountain ridge where
she'd run with sundogs in the solar fields.

Now even on cold days she stands at the cliffs,
looking out to sea in such a way that her eyes

can't see the ground beneath her feet.
Sometimes she can feel her wings growing.

Birdwatcher

For seven years I've tried to approach the ground zero
of my neighborhood, which happens to be the nation's,
my daily walk to work, for a long time, through allies
of wreckage, detours that couldn't circle wider
than the stench of burning flesh, and though
the rubble was carried off and quotidian alarms
sounded the all-clear, the horns triggering explosives
to sink new foundations, the dwelling of our
persistent belief in a future, and my own, the ribs
of the new station arcing like a nest, I wake to a life
still at the edge of ruins, a train snaking round the pit
to disgorge its passengers onto a platform, its length
overlapped in the fog of histories, like the long approach
to Athena's throne, or the Via Appia, but paved over,
stairs at the end rising to the fences, which lead me
round the rim, walking into the low, autumn sun
pressing metallic foil to the bell towers of St. Paul's
and Trinity Church, slowly lifting its head above rooftops,
stretching its fingers through streets, poking the Hudson,
seeming to search with a birdwatcher's quiet caution
for a glimpse of the shadows it can cast but never catch.

Learning How to Hunger

I have to spend a little time studying the shadows
of railings and benches. I need a half hour each day
to follow the arguments of scrounging sparrows
and leaves turning over in the crosswalks.

No matter what time of year, there's always
one or two there declaiming the true philosophy.

And when I pick out a new tree to love,
one to replace those first loves of youth,
I'll choose the one outside my house, the one
I've tried so many times to identify, following
the shape of its leaves, the type of its blossoms,
but have failed. The hairy acorn of a bur oak,
the toothed leaf of a beech—none of them lead
to a name that gives me the right to say *I know you*.

My wife curses it for the catkins
littering the sidewalk like withered hourglasses.
All summer its arms cool my stoop with shade,
though it's the nameless power of its bark
that arches over me where I sit
gnawing its roots and curiosities,
growing strong with hunger.

Feeding the Chameleon

Chameleons stroll the promenade along the Hudson—
hundreds of them coloring themselves
with misgiving, no two alike—
some mauve, some morose, some sobbing.
I think they aren't my kind of animal,
but here I am with them watching the waves
shuffle and the gray sky, and waiting
as I have been

for a mouth, scrounging for words,
words that mean
I am at war with rain and its legion of puddles,
that light is a history of slow cooling,
and all the people puzzling over their private narratives
are less honest than the marble,
than its conglomeration of spotty boils
colored black, tan, and ash.

I feed one of the chameleons a cricket
and watch him bleed into the bench beside me.
Then I watch the Hudson pass in its flashing brown skirts.
I hum a bit of a Prokofiev sonata, scratch a note
about tourists snapping shots of themselves,
this need to say *I'm here.*
I scratch at the paint on the bench, scratch
at every surface until I find something
for which I won't ask to be forgiven.

The Reservoir

For years people slaked their thirst
at the source of things,
syphoned off the top layer of water,
just what reflected their needs back to them
and the endless blue into which they expanded.

But the colossus of their desires outgrew it
and they turned to feed off deeper tunnels,
from pipelines that burrowed and reached
through the dark muck beyond the city limits.

Meanwhile the reservoir continued to collect
their neglected time, feeding wild grasses,
tufted marsh flowers, black cherry trees,
and the rare animals of their abandoned lives,
nesting in every moist and forgotten corner.

In later seasons people returned to paddle
through its waters, to cut paths around its shores
and preserve something they could only express
as a walk in the hot swelter of nostalgias,

or fishing under the shadow of its Romanesque
pump stations, which rose on either side
like silent, rotting bell towers, so that sometimes
far from the shoreline, from a bed

of algae patterns and shaded patches, a line
would catch some wild and peculiar thing,
familiar as déjà vu, a cold, scaly hint
at the name they once answered to.

The Infinite Doctrine of Water

Go around, it says, or through or under or over,
but go on.

Stand still for no one and no thing,
because when you stop,

your breath will thicken and grow dark,
the life swimming in you

rot. The stones will not preserve you,
their hands will not endure; in fact, you will grind

them down to pepper the way for those who follow.
Whatever trinkets you pick up,

soften them in your hands, shaping them
with the gentle art of friction,

for whatever is worth carrying is worth
imprinting with the change you are

part of. And remember to drop them
somewhere along the way to the sea,

small polished pieces of you
left behind to collect the light.

Bioluminescence

Old philosophers would call this look *melancholia*,
but I see in this photo of my wife thinking
weathers of competing beauty,
someone who can be in two places at once:
there on the couch, leaning into the cushion folds,
and somewhere else focused on the unseen,
beyond the clock's exhausting rap,
working an idea like dough into the necessary bread.

All moments of clarity narrow like this,
the periphery dimmed as in a Rembrandt,
his "Philosopher in Meditation" sitting in a shaft of light
as if at the bottom of a well, because the profound
leads into dark places, like the ocean floor where
the only illumination comes from the bodies of fish
swimming through its miles of perpetual night.

Turpentine

I might be late to meet a friend because I want to listen
to bacon repeat its delicious static in the kitchen,
or stand at the window looking into the yard,
trying to decipher the hieroglyphs of shadow
stenciled in the carpet of dead leaves, or hear them
tapping together in wind like a collection of beads,
wondering what each color signifies, each sound,
or I might stay up late again, noting different shades of dark,
the variant tones of a distant train here in Jersey City
blending with traffic, steam pipes, and stray cats
huddled under cars for warmth, and how this weave
differs from what I remember in Pennsylvania
carried in the heavy chill through sugar maples,
like a thread wound and unwound in their limbs,
and how these two versions of a distant train are distant
from each other, divergent farther down their tracks
than can be seen at any point along the way, or hinted at
in their cargos, or understood by their schedules, because
they travel circuits of private meaning, intimate as memories,
like those of my uncles who were carpenters, who hammered
and painted their lives out of wood and wallpaper,
and filled their refrigerators with mason jars of turpentine,
brush handles poking up like wooden beaks, the acrid smell
filling the house with what I remember as the power of revision.

II

New Pens

Every year I buy new pens because I like the idea
of new ink, black ink like a dark, clotted insight
about to bleed onto paper, like a brilliance that burns
with threatening in the windows, that allows
no passengers along its glowing tracks
because fire is more than what it illuminates,
more than rose hips, hibiscus, and baby bok choy
thrown like a still-life onto the kitchen table,
or corbels shouldering the granite mantel,
the way what we are is more than what we do,
carried into the day by a deeper thrust in our veins
and in our viscera, a more forceful pulse
pushing a jagged key into locks, opening the way
to back alleys and intrusions of thought
falling like snow that traces a wall face,
the gray stone protrusions, the white spelling out,
in cold cursive, the granite disclosures of endurance
and regard, as flakes fill in the keyhole on a gate,
and frame in the bars a path through an ice garden.

Cipher

On the long road home I stopped for gas.
Behind the station
         small, black chimney swifts
circled at the edge of a farm field. As they
spiraled up and dove,
         they seemed to tease out
from the corn stalks strands of sunlight,
as if to bundle them
         into gold sheaves,
store them for the nighttime thrifts, the ones
who struggle
         with the old translations,
the right words to negotiate the divides:
body and mind,
         the dark and its habitations,
the drama of a story and all it implies.
It's an ancient manuscript,
         sometimes
in a primordial language. But as I drove off,
I was happy
         if not content, to have
this new version of the text to consider,
trying to decipher
         over the years
who wrote it and what it all meant.

Study for Infatuation

Sometimes the blue sky threatens,
the lilac conceals some danger.
But it passes like a cougar
stalking among the boulders
and deciding mysteriously
to move on. You don't know,
but something you did
or didn't do, saved your life.

And what might have happened
had you turned your back
on this sunset, this rotting
fence post, this dandelion
dripping its yellow
into the cracks along the gutter?

Something seamlessly escapes
and you can't follow. Sealed away
in the loam and marrow, its tracks
evaporate like water and like water,
when again it dashes a flirtatious spindrift
before you, it will mass, a cloud over trees
seeming fresh with such an allure
shading the street, an enticement
of flight and melody, it will play
in the mind like an etude, strength
to endure the long, beautiful devouring.

Learning to Read the Ice

The day is leaving, or wandering off to a corner
of the goose field, keeping its secret at a safe distance,
low in the ginger grass and cold, its waves tucked
in leaf folds and the hard retreating hills, or slipping
at the curbs through sewer grates or backwards
up weathered facades, the clean variation
of suburban homes, already practiced in warmth.
Even with the great letdown of maple leaves
patching lawns and raked drifts in the streets,
it's not a giving up but a holding back, holding on,
a way of enduring, persisting in this landscape,
this earth of early days, scenes of adolescent walks,
the groping through afterthoughts, through odors
of decline, circling the lake, sifting its iced rim
for a hint, a clue to its hard, cold economies.

Spy Game

There's an entry in the sidewalk's journal today
scripted in rainwater and legible only as a flash
passing under headlights.

There's another stenciled in the milky reflections of windows
and another down the street,
brushed in currents of the Hudson's gray ink.

Such epiphanies accumulate in gutters and drains,
the margins of everyday disorder.

I write them in a notebook to decipher later,
to see the letters in their message darken
like the lemon juice on those notes I wrote when I was young,
pretending to be a spy, risking his life to keep a secret.

Reading for Pleasure

I sometimes—no, often—have to say things out loud
to understand them because that voice in my head
doesn't sound like me, doesn't know that words
have hard textures like a canvas bag or wool sweater
that need to be rubbed roughly to make sense and he
is a too clean-shaven idea about me to really get
what I'm about, with flaky skin that crusts around my nose
when I don't wash regularly, roughage shading my cheek
on days without a razor and how wise and forgiving
the mere rhythm of language can be, like a stress ball
that's more comforting tossed in the air than squeezed,
feeling its heft and fall, its body slapping the palm when it
comes back down, as all things do, even stinging, as if to blast
the lines in the hand and reroute them, change the schedule,
the mapping and the simple work that a hand can do, like
pointing through a window or beyond the anchoring ground,
past familiar oceanic weights and measures, toward something
like an interruption, as when we reclined on a beach at midnight
and one flash of bioluminescence hyphenated the breakers
making the dark into a thick scribble of text, where an aqueous
editor tested the buoyancy of each rewrite, and we sat back,
silent the rest of the night, watching for the next revision,
mindless of the final version and who, in the end, would own it.

Sage

None of my dictionaries define it as a color
and yet my wife tells me it's the color
of our wedding—her dress, my tie.

I take her word for it, but feel no wiser.

I sometimes find it in the tiles of some mosaic
or fired into a mug now on clearance at the store
and I'm suddenly connected, rooted,

though it depends on the light, as color always does,
changing with air densities and angles,
shifting with the hours, aging

like the plant that is this color's namesake,
its leaves like fingers pointing in every direction,
as if it knew something.

Surfacing

It's a day when one can hear
        the morning glories growing,
inching in their curls through the fences,
        a kind of rip and snap.

Things buried leach to the surface:
        the scratch and shuffle of a woodchuck
tunneling beneath our yard
        simmers up through the autumn leaves,
and crickets crawl out
        from under basement trashcans.
Bone fragments at Ground Zero
        are hauled into the afternoon air.

Their marrows cored
        by five years of decay,
these nuggets of the past,
        sifted out of the quotidian,
still glitter with the weight
        of the day they were buried,
a metal precious enough
        to transfix any observer.

Unanswered questions return
        with the regularity of the photographer's
golden time, the persistence of shadow
        lengthening toward the ideal moment,
which is so hard to believe in and yet,
        even the papers report the next day
how a man on a beach discovered
        a bag of unopened letters in the water,

all of them prayers addressed to God.

Scraps

I throw on a trench coat and tuck
my pen inside the breast pocket
only to pull out an old ticket stub for Paris
or the birth plan of our first child,
the day dissolved into another lifetime,
my fork slicing a square of foi gras
in the Crémerie-Restaurant Polidor,
bumping elbows with the ghosts of André Gide,
Valéry, and Joyce, or in Florence, turning
from the Palazzo Vecchio toward the Arno
and wondering if this might be a corner
where Dante paused to consider his Beatrice,
or staying awake the 27th straight hour
to talk my wife through her next contraction,
as today I talk myself through the monotony
and my failure to discard and organize,
leaving scraps tucked away like receipts
of a life lived in reckless wonder.

The Generosity of the Past

In our apartment there was always light
splitting through the windows like mercy,
illuminating bookshelves and what we thought,
our conversations or our glasses of wine
lifted to toast each day of generosity:
the quantity surpassing what we knew.

We read our books, discussed the world we knew,
interpretations shifting with the light.
We lived by an aesthetic of generosity,
art and music painting our world with mercy,
although diluted by several bottles of wine
and so reduced to memory and thought.

Sediment in the bottles was like a thought,
a remnant of the past and all we knew:
nights listening to Liszt or tasting wine,
arguing over how things changed with light,
how sometimes saying nothing is like mercy,
and disagreeing was a generosity.

The simplest things are forms of generosity:
like paying bills, or making tea with thought
for how you like it: sugar, a little mercy.
We knew that once but then forgot we knew.
So when we changed we blamed the changing light,
and turned to vinegar like aging wine.

But then we'd drink just anything: old wine,
bad scotch, tequila. Though still generosity,
a generosity that took no delight,
not in our books, not in a word or thought.
We toasted to the past and what we knew,
began the long goodbyes with little mercy.

If time allowed us to forgive, that's mercy.
And I recall with every glass of wine
because it's who I am and what I knew
and I am thankful for the generosity
of that time, for its store of meaning and thought,
which are to me here now a kind of light:

for it's a light that makes a spectrum of mercy,
colorful thoughts as deep and rich as wine,
a generosity that's always new.

Setting Fires

We sat in the kitchen talking about tomatillos,
that they were the distilled essence of all that's repulsive
in tomatoes and I stared into the table
trying to remember the philosophical word
for what makes something what it is, one of those
memory lapses I'm told increases with age
and dogs me now that I'm about to turn forty.
Just then I imagined a bat flapping into the kitchen
and attacking me. It must have been what pursued me
into another day that was just as desperate,
driving through the Catskill mountains, late again,
closed roads, wrong turns, and houses where
no one answered the doors and autumn leaves burned
in the backyards. It had something to do with choices made
and not being able to turn back and the smoke
of those burning leaves torn by wind into nothing
except a sweet, dissipating aroma accenting the hills.

Counting Apples

Entering Zuccotti Park, I pass through nearly leafless
shade of honey locust, over an incline of pink granite
scuffed and dulled by deepening cold, by
the dry clarities and harsh abandonments of autumn
often mistaken for oblivion, the way it pours
into the smallest cracks, widening the divides,
the way our friend's birthday party escapes me
even as you recite its details—the salsa music,
the dancing, the prix fixe menu—or someone else asks
if I've seen *My Dinner with Andre* since watching it
back in the early 90's, and I can't recall, and suddenly
I feel poor, a victim of theft and swing my hand hard,
slapping a limb overhead, a pathetic rebellion
that shakes a few leaves loose, dancing down
around me like a yellow insight,
a brilliance passed on as a realization that
I hadn't seen a butterfly all summer and wouldn't
now that it was over and I was filled with regret
and the need to walk up to the Farmer's stand
and count the different types of apple for sale—
gala, golden delicious, red delicious, granny smith,
mutsu—eleven in all, eleven different shapes earth gave
to its memories, eleven different shapes of praise.

III

Treading Water

Wind warps the Hudson's tide line, shuffling
waves like cards in a magic trick. Though it's clear
the deck is stacked, it isn't clear in whose favor:
the sun poking the crests or the gulls
who circle back in hungry ambivalence
almost seeming cued to retreat by the prows,
the nodding boats at dock and even those
hesitating at the outlet, where rivers plunge
into the wide expanse of Atlantic salt, currents
like hundreds of fingers wagging at the fluidity
of the historic, the generosity of chance, where
once Hamlet thought a while in pelagic sweeps
that someday he too would play the role of Yorik,
a thought as common as water, and blinding,
like this radiant body, a brilliant armor
covering the deep where fish and white crabs
sift the murk, the thick muddy limits of what is known,
unsettling the locked riches of the dark bottom
into a string of rising aqueous rungs,
stirring the upper decks, where another gull
prowls the shuffling surfaces, and dives.

Renewing My Passport

Every day I have to decide when to cut over
to Broadway, as if choosing a theme,
maybe the expedient dash up Fulton Street
bordered by the iron fence of St. Paul's Church,
gravestones blinking through the posts.

But with no way to dodge the crowds,
Cortlandt Street suggests a way between
the polished granite of Century 21
and Liberty Plaza's silver skyscraper,
its vitreous wall seeming to slide with shoppers.

When the days are liquid, it's best to pass on,
if only to the next block, where I can take
a diagonal across Zuccotti Park, idiosyncratic
except when passed under the legs
of its *Joie de Vivre* sculpture, red and angled
like calipers, which I avoid when I don't want
the width of my luck measured,

so I can skip over instead to Thames Street,
up its narrow alley, between Big Al's Pizza
and the Suspenders Bar and Restaurant, feeling,
as I always do on small streets, transported
to some Florentine corner, or a Parisian market,
if only for the way, in summer, it's sometimes
closed off, a carpet thrown down and chairs put out,
if only for feeling lost again among possibilities.

Close Reading

I used to read while nestled in a crook
of maple branches, or seated on a slab of concrete
that jutted into lake water,
striders coasting the rumpled sheets.

Reeds on the far shore needled the shallows
writing a subtext into palms of sunlight
alluding to trout and bass tunneling the deep,
to the early alphabets of mud and rock.

Mallards skirted the surface by day,
bats skimmed it by night, their wings
scratching brief calligraphies into the water.
There was always something to read,

a word or glyph to decipher: Canada geese
pausing in their long migrations,
or a dead fish with pierced armor
leaking his guts to the summer sun,

to flies unzipping the air
in busy gratitude, to those days
when my idea of heaven was so big
it contained even this.

Chain Links

Immensities open between the summer maple
and fence. I could live ten thousand lives
and not enter them all. So I give everything
to take notice, abandon every plan that doesn't chase
the retreating realities down into their stones,
retrieve some nugget from the random shallows,
from afternoon brilliance dressing them in a rich promise
of storm clouds and convulsive rain.

Gray pulses crackle like a burning in the collage
that is Jersey City: dogwoods and parking lots,
mulberries and factory pipes threaded like circuitry,
high platforms where the downpour's reconnaissance
pulls back, heaves its weathers into the sky,

its lofty history legible now in the muddy gutters
and flooded basements. Although it's only in
the aqueous pearls strung through the fence, massing
in the chain links, where I notice an identity
scattered but equal in every sack
and sufficient to cup the day's fading visions.

Fire Eater

What could the stars have meant
never aligning with your routines
or sugaring your coffee with direction?

All that energy wasted, the soup cans,
the leaking batteries filling dreams
with a stockpile of ruins, reminders
of how clocks once ticked and pushed on.

Though it's not that sad: the scarf
tighter around your neck, the sky
an ice blue grinder of gusty intentions,
shredding the air into folds clouding over:

each crease of coat lining, each crack
in the street, where the cold mysteriously
ripples, a wake you pass through
gathering every last drifting flake of radiance,

compressed inside you until your heart catches fire.

How a Bridge Is Built

The Devil envied God his power;
I envy his attention to detail
down to the mitochondria
by whose cellular fires I warm myself.

To be aware of every speck of dust—
that is to truly live—be a master of minutiae,
every marginal memory, like that day in winter
wind stirred day-old snow into the air,
flakes glinting like tinsel
                                      and I knew
I missed something, that part of me was missing,
off constructing a bridge between that confetti

and the day before when I passed a bar
where some red balloons capped in snow
sank under the weight, like minds heavy with insights,

how, at first, I had no idea what they were,
that they looked like something out of a children's tale,
a radioactive fungus where a giant mantis sat
drunk with wisdom, spoke a language that connected it all,

and I could almost understand.

Collecting Coins

Because others seem to remember my life
better than I do, because I never pretended
I could win the wager, but from the start said
to every moment, *stay, you're so beautiful*,
because the family history doesn't go back
beyond the 20th century, though I've been told
my great-great grandmother could only speak
Pennsylvania Dutch and some grandfather beyond
invented the merry-go-round, which is a lie, because
I've learned it was invented by Louis XIV and I see
how one of my uncles built every house he's lived in
because it's a way of creating a story out of wood
and cement, a foundation to replace the traditions
and histories we never had or forgot to write down,
because the stories are all like the coin dug up
from the dirt basement in my grandparent's house:
gold, antique, worth enough to make the whole
family rich, if only some expert would say it's real.

Counting Change

The moon this morning lingers
above the industrial landscape,
a coin paying my passage into the day.

How much it costs to get to the next moment,
how high the price was to arrive here
from all the way back when I was seven,
collecting coins and holding a liberty nickel from 1884,
worth a few dollars, and wishing it were
just one year younger and worth so much more,
and feeling how the value of that year
would weigh in my hand, a nickel
worth three hundred dollars,
how it meant something then

that today, thirty-six years later, means
this moon is so beautiful and bright
I stand and just look, and am late for work,
and keep the bosses waiting.

Private Constellations

I keep finding what others leave behind:
a change purse at a bus stop, a book
on a newel post, a scarf on a stoop.

These abandonments trace constellations,
figures in the dark sky of a story
we no longer tell each other.

Sometimes a clue surfaces like a feeling about
what I should order from the menu, leaving
five minutes later for work, or seeing a different movie.

But because disparate solutions accumulate,
the puzzle remains unsolved, and I find myself
randomly discarding things: maybe a pen

left on some café table and leaving with it
my wish on the star that it might become
in the story of someone else's telling.

The Longest Hibernation

I once collected notebooks of runes and hieroglyphs,
traced the evolving stages of Chinese from pictograms
to ideograms, felt their swoops and curls under my hand
as if the pen were a key about to unlock a cage
releasing some mythical bird, a kindled emissary
beating about the room, striking some fire, nesting
habitably as the barns nested in the hills and farms
of Oley, their spotted hex signs, their haylofts thick
with fodder and secrets molting in the rafters,
all of it forked down the feeding holes to the cattle
with the necessity of full disclosure and endurance.
Or that's how it would turn out in our favorite stories,
those that fed the slow progress to the better life
even then, in the 70s, when my Uncle Woody
worked in a glass factory, could only say he had
made domes for missile silos, but nothing more,
all the details vitreous, greased, and in our best interest,
like the Cold War, like the triple triangle on the school
across the street, a sign, a symbol so blunt
it was the opposite of shelter, a place to burrow down
like an animal curling into a long hibernation,
trying to sleep through the end of everything.

Devotional

At times the soul needs to crouch in its
cramped corners and scoop dust into piles,
feeling warm as a hamster under its woodchips.

At others, it needs to cut loose, divorce
itself from the intimate rooms of its sleep,
travel the long interstate toward damp fields,

like that along New York Bay, I-278, the Belt Parkway
toward the Verrazano Narrows Bridge, its arches
long and elegant as a young wife's finger pointing north
through a haze sifting sunbeams over the river
coating Manhattan's glass towers in cream.

In the distance between, ranks of waves
wear breakers like medals of impermanence,
honors of their brevity accented
by gulls shrieking and thick air salted with sea,

a severance of all ties to the land's thrift,
like waking from a long hibernation to inhale
the sky's vacancies, filling the lungs with its
crisp absence, its capacity to hold nothing back.

IV

Breadcrumbs

I keep believing in the fresh start,
keep turning back as if to begin,
but there's no going past the push of hunger.

As a child, I filled jugs at a natural spring,
my hands rich with the scent of moss,
the rocks gurgling, the smell of wet soil
saturating the air with a kind of habitable baptism,
a slaked freshness I rose from
                              and turned toward home.

Years later, as I pass a construction site
and each morning there's a little more cement,
a few more girders, wiring and steel
fused under acetylene flies,
I realize all those hands, all those minds

pick their way through halls of carbon and fly ash,
trace potentials down molecular paths of iron,
water and gravel, bits and pieces like breadcrumbs
trailing all the way back to subterranean lavas
and prehistoric furnaces, the inhuman fires
that go into making every habitation and home.

How We Learn

Over rivers and lakes, far from our familiar porches,
the weight of the day massed and crept toward us.
It was a part of nature's lesson plan, the measure
of a chemical reaction between time and meaning,
since the beakers all bubbled and something waited
to happen, though no one waited for it to happen,
like bushes in a city park shaking with the first song
of a newborn bird, unwinding only for the slow-moving
and subterranean, submerged in soliloquies of earth tones
and the darkness of the day's last hours, those
that slate windows to the receptive black of chalkboards
absorbing the stenciled homework assignment
into the weather of a student's first nostalgias,
the gray drifts and rain that turn like thick pages in his sleep,
forces that pound into him, all night, a seismic knowledge.

Some Cracks

Some cracks can't be mended and some shouldn't be,
like those on the mountain roads of childhood,
at the edge of a sheer drop, where the gray stone walls
split under years of drumming rain, and from them

honeysuckle poked out toward the sky and golden rod,
over treetops into the smoldering aromas of summer
and youth, the rooted weathers of memory and invention,
because even these lines sprouted from its image,

and the sweet yellows swelled to the old fire outpost,
the lookout tower at the crest of the mountain from where,
in every direction, it was all downhill, cycling toward
the close of the year when every trail burned, reaching

all the way to the autumn corn, the farm fields,
the starved leaves of honey locust, silver maple, ginkgo,
and white ash, the foliate silhouette of the mountain
stripped to bare branches against the sky, looking like cracks

veined through blue flint glass, the deep crevices of bark
hardened against the cold in a posture of endurance, the roots
clinging to choked soil, crust of a genuine promise.

What It Was Like

There was a moment I think I meant something else,
when the epiphanies came without hesitations and
second guesses, without the slowing effects of rain
and snow, their deepening doubletalk or precipitous white,

when I walked at a pace in tune not only
with the red flash through autumn leaves and those
incalculable jittery descents, but with cabs swerving
off Broadway, with a subway's halts and jumps
through dark tunnels, a discarded bag jolted upward
on invisible pressures, water fanned from fire hydrants,
those stubby symbols of a belief that something can be saved.

Time was there were other ways of becoming, when
generosity meant thankfulness even in desolate times,
even in the dry, gold weed hanging from cracks,
deepening autumn toward winter in the cold gray stone,
or a puddle down a narrow alley, its reflection
a single point of illumination enriching the dark,
the way I stared into the dread, seized it, and became whole.

After Rain

After rain it's possible to forgive, to accept
the random potential for depth, scattered
everywhere in puddles, the shining danger
of leaves on roads and sidewalks, the luster
of disjointed umbrella spokes in the gutter,
because nothing profound is safe. That's why
its chasms are hoarded or pawned in each drop,
streaked, dragged down building facades,
beaded in windows, swallowed in the drains.

It's the high price of reflection and, in the city
especially, our grandest gestures, the arcs
of intention double in aqueous miniature,
slick the soles of our shoes making them slip
and squeak, forcing reconsiderations
of the melodramatic, its potential for injury
or regret, as if the sea gods, even on this
small scale, will not weather our indifferences
and ambitions, knowing we can drown
in an inch of water and tomorrow, though
the sun will heat the puddles, as the waters
shrivel in the rising temperature, the sun's image
will shrink, slowly going under, sinking
beyond reach and comprehension.

Tuning In

There are rhythms even to hesitations and missteps,
cracked and caving sidewalks, moments in the dark
before a noonday storm when streetlights snap on
and the clock hands skid into the green dark of reversals

like sitting with my father at the kitchen table explaining
how to end his need to make me a symbol of his losses,
another symbol with his receipts scattered among beer bottles
and bottle caps, a few slipping under the toaster oven,

as if the heating coils summoned the past to its burning,
drawing the dates into their domestic fires
because we grow old in what we know, because
such coals will last the winter, warming the house
to the windows, to the glass edge of what I am,

holding at the sills, staring into the dark,
buzzing like a radio in a static search for a signal.

A Remaining Shot

I grew up with shale as a tongue, chipped and black
as a chalkboard, and thus I was marked by place,
and marked by every transition from maple slopes
in eastern Pennsylvania to the industrial avenues
of Jersey City, abandoned factories remade as condos,
ramps to truck routes extending like mycelium,
trails veined like a shattered surface, a memory
of shifting maps, directions changed by one slip
turning the past to regret or nostalgia, images
sliding like lenses flipped by an optometrist,
*How does that look? And how about that? Better
or worse? Better or worse?* A marriage of sorts.
The clean slate cracked irreparably when I splashed
in a fountain behind the Congressional offices in DC,
or woke the next morning, light stripped down to green,
a remaining shot of chartreuse on the floor, the drive
home, a car engulfed in flames on the side of route 95,
fires as tall as the surrounding trees, rooted, thirsting,
like me, sitting back in the car to drink it all in.

Below Deck

Waking to a gray leviathan of cumulus drifting eastward
and a late morning downpour, it seems the November gods
are displaced ocean deities, raging for some Odysseus
that lives in a tree, shaking the summer closets,

rattling the chambers down to bare bark and bone,
the ruthless honesties and precipitous disclosures
everywhere like dead leaves, a phone call from someone
never met, the news of a friend's fatal stroke falling like

another autumnal devastation, the dogwoods and sycamores
in deep trenches of regret, wagging their boney fingers,
the *what-ifs* and *I-should-haves*. Strange how the harbingers
of these revelations are doomed to repeat themselves,

even the greatest among them were enslaved to fate,
as reckless as weather and as indifferent,
which the Greeks knew, and Plato condemned them for,
because compassion is rooted in earth like trees,

or men, equally balding, wizened, standing on a pier
discussing ships at dock, cargoes fished from accident,
from lost intentions, stored below deck in the mind
with the fortunes of hazard and bounties of risk.

My Jersey City

The sun rises from trees, its glory
pooling under the leaves. But only for a moment,

then the wind shakes it loose, glinting along rails
as a train pulls out from Journal Square

passing a recess in the granite trench
where a ginkgo twists like a dancer of green grace

fixed in a precarious balance between revelation
and mystery, which it passes on like love, never content

to stay in the same place long, and maybe changes
with each arrival, now billowing from smokestacks

off Pulaski Skyway, now falling through car fumes
in the wake of a swooping gull.

Its avenues through the swampy stench of mildew
bless even the collapsed docks rotting in shore water

bursting the terms of beauty and disclosure
with the plumes of fireworks at Liberty State Park.

It travels the same dark bridges as the pounding rain
reaching down to the roots where it settles and waits.

Seed

I prefer reading history
in a flowering of dirt
and cooked mud,
the glittering text
of macadam after rain,
the squirrel's risky
acrobatics in the mulberry,
leaps from limb to limb
to telephone cables,
the occasional fall and
hard thud. The beauty
of this daring makes a stage
of my backyard, makes
the page of a story printed
in the very enactment,
an image I carry with me,
like a book of hours
or the stained glass panels
of Sainte Chapelle, telling
the whole story from creation
to the end of the world
in images and colors
radiant with struggle.

Chestnut

On this late April day, all the dormant powers
    break into their first green disclosures,
        digging out from under rocks,

surging up from circuits of soil and sap,
    dirt, darkness and the deep cold water tables,
        holding out the early seasonal revelations:

hyacinth and tulip, magnolia, and dogwood.
    Around the fountains and park benches they rewrite
        the long history from the first day until now,

an unfolding accented by sweet aromas that remind me
    memory is another flowering of imagination,
        seductive as any other beauty and why

I can't seem to throw away a chestnut
    snatched from the floor of late October colors
        and since then, palmed in my pocket,

its smooth woodiness under my thumb, its hard promise
    like an elegant refusal, the friction against my finger,
        an integrity that yields to nothing but its own terms.

v

Like Rain

The rain in the dark is making its way somewhere,
a barely noticeable pulse, shoving a dim flash.
Something snaps into place and I remember
where I left the keys, and so, it's a returning,
like those famous flying buttresses of Notre Dame
carrying all that weight down into dirt, the deep
immovable murk. Thus the walls have stood
for centuries, and we step back in the afternoon sun
admiring the grandeur of it, the way it all seems
to rise and write itself in the hot summer air,
a suggestion of wings and ethereal choirs,
or a simpler image of someone sitting at a window,
looking out, his eyes traveling the length of interstate
into a distance of cables and sloping hills, trees
and warehouses, an intersection of descending arcs
where his thought gathers in puddles like rain
settling to the bottom, into the lowest basin where
it retraces its precipitous path: a reflection without regret.

Following the Clues

I'm a day behind every day, trying to catch the sun's tail,
which is actually lunar, curved and marbled, cold,

indifferent to something like the 7th prelude & fugue
of Shostakovich, which nearly breaks my heart, and this chase

has left me a caffeine addict stuttering at the keys
into what used to be called the mirknight, an obsolete

but beautiful, muddy word for the darkest time of night,
when conversations have unctuous momentum,

the way we once talked until your apartment darkened,
never moving to turn on a lamp or get a drink, as if we were

about to overtake something just ahead of us, something
that would utterly change us, and maybe did, as I return

to this memory that's now grainy like a stylized photo,
seeming fixed in an album with others, next to this one

of tomatoes picked from the garden for our sandwiches,
and this one on the corner of Broadway and 12th Street

where I hold a copy of Pasternak's autobiography,
each image surfacing like a clue.

Tailor-made

Fog fell like fabric from the top shelf,
remainders of fleece and gabardine
fitted for the ground and buildings:

the Jersey Journal's facade and doors,
the H&R Block sign in the window,
every arch and sidewalk trimmed,

bonded to a bottom layer of gauze
so nothing could be seen
beyond the middle of the street

and even the late night's darkness
waxed and cracked, gray and white
batik. And under the sheets

streetlights ghosted the avenues, railings
were shaved off before the top step
where all passed into primordial memory,

a prenatal comfort so dense even a mother
couldn't fabricate its warmth and promise:
this could be anywhere and you could be anyone.

Paperclip

I learned that in an interview to enter Oxford
they might ask how you would describe infinity,
and I thought about once being asked
how I would describe a paperclip to an alien,
that is, to someone who's never seen one.
It was a writing exercise that made me think
of how I would describe the autumn mountains
where I grew up, and I decided that they
are the color of whiskey and intoxication,
and exuberance, which might be a way
of describing a paperclip, that is, a wire
that's intoxicated, wandering in circles,
swiveling on its heels as it makes its way out
to meet friends that it embraces, holds together
in a maudlin circle of endearment,
all of which is also how I think of the infinite.

Bless the Scavengers

At the horizon, the November sun harvests a crop
of yesterdays and pierces the bus's windows
all the way to the Square, at every intersection,

a flash of emblazoned silhouettes, a clock tower,
telephone wires beaded with fiery birds,
mist dampening skyscrapers at the harbor edge,

their sterling glass kindled in the cold salt air,
vague and burning like a palimpsest
on which the day is about to be written, shimmering

with conflicts, the possibilities of misdirected traffic,
delayed trains, flooded tunnels, or bomb threats.
Although the avenues along this route are not yet

indelible, as long as the mist clings to the streets,
as long as the perspective's scoured by dry leaves,
autumn trees wag their limbs and gulls strafe

wrenching morsels of decay from gutters
and rooftop tiles, like scavenging angels,
clearing the way for a season of second chances.

Signature

All the leaves have dropped and cover the stiff, dry grass,
a loose littering of golds, browns, and maroons,
an aesthetically pleasing mess, or plates of armor cast
from the furnaces of Hephaestus under the aegis of stray cats
slinking through the underbrush at the yard's edge,
where the slope is sudden and steep, down to the avenue,
lined with gas stations, motels, chemical plants,
and one cemetery, gated, preserved against the other ensigns
of the 21st century, because a cemetery is never dated.
Like the one you pass on long drives through Pennsylvania,
a plot of ground no more than thirty by thirty feet,
fenced in by a low stone wall, a spot surrounded
by slopes of furrowed farmland, the quilted contract
the mind has with earth, randomly signed with thanksgiving,
with variation in the landscape's theme, with continuity
of its promises and resolutions, a kind of rising and falling,
a kind of curving and pressing on, like hills,
like a signature sweeping the page and reaching as far
as the kitchen this morning that was filled with the smell
of bacon fat and coffee, comforts as warm as the worn coat
you wrapped yourself in, to take your son to run through the leaves.

Peculiar Smoke

The smell of clove cigarettes climbed the escalators
carried in a basket of nostalgias
bound to its claustrophobic weave as tight as our studio
back in the summer of 1990
where I first tasted that peculiar smoke,
three of us living in one room for the sake of art,
love, and adventure, the August heat an impossible weight
dripping from us like a future rooted in New York streets
until it called itself home.
It was a summer of brandy, sex, and poetry,
when we believed in nothing except our passions
and obsessions and picked at the one loose thread
in the tapestry, its story unraveled
until no one could remember how it went,
only, here and there, a little color, a bit of scenery,
a shaft of summer cloud like a support beam
running under the floor of tomorrow's weather,
a passage of music threading reflections in the window
and making sense of it all only years later
in the click of an escalator,
its cycle of rotating belts and collapsing steps
carrying me up and down and through
the long, circular days.

The Voice of Water

It sounds like grape leaves shaking.
It cushions like thick grass underfoot.
Its currents spread beyond the range of mountains

which is why sometimes people mistake it
for the distant trickle of the sun setting.
The error depends on which way they're walking—

and if the wind is blowing from the north or south.
It licks your fingers when you wave and only by its tongue
can you tell if the person you're greeting is a stranger

or some distant uncle. Comforted by one
of its many dialects, your neighbor
grins from his porch, cigarette in hand.

When it whispers, it whispers with
the same heaping hush of salt
pouring from an uncapped shaker.

Because of its excesses it remembers.
Even after you've closed the book
it keeps reciting the lines.

Acknowledgments

Grateful acknowledgment is made to the following journals in which the poems in this collection first appeared:

The Adirondack Review: "Turpentine"
Askew: "Bioluminescence"
Barn Owl Review: "Contrast"
Barrow Street: "Learning to Read the Ice"
Coe Review: "Peculiar Smoke"
Construction: "Chestnut"
Fogged Clarity: "Breadcrumbs," "Close Reading," "My Jersey City," "Paperclip"
The Good Men Project: "Counting Change"
Hypothetical: "Scraps"
Iodine Poetry Journal: "After Rain, "New Pens," "Some Cracks"
Ithaca Lit: "Cipher," "Devotional"
Jellyroll: "Like Rain," "Spy Game"
The Jersey City Independent: "The Infinite Doctrine of Water"
The Literary Bohemian: "Renewing My Passport"
Loch Raven Review: "Birdwatcher"
MadHat Annual: "A Remaining Shot"
Mayday: "Study for Infatuation," "The Voice of Water"
The Meadowland Review: "Counting Apples"
Möbius: "Following the Clues"
Newtown Literary: "Signature"
NYCBigCityLit: "Chain Links," "How We Learn"
Off the Coast: "Advice from a Bat," "Molting," "Tuning In"
The Raintown Review: "Setting Fires"
The Red Wheelbarrow: "Fire Eater," "The Reservoir," "Treading Water"
River Oak Review: "The Longest Hibernation"
The Same: "Collecting Coins," "Feeding the Chameleon," "Learning How to Hunger"
Scythe: "Below Deck"
Poetry Quarterly: "Bless the Scavengers," "Surfacing," "What It Was Like"
Think Journal: "The Generosity of the Past"

Tiferet: "Seed"
Tribeca Poetry Review: "Private Constellations," "Sage"
Upstreet: "Reading for Pleasure"
Waccamaw: "How a Bridge is Built"

"Advice from a Bat" was reprinted in *The Crafty Poet: A Portable Workshop*, ed. Diane Lockward (Wind Publications, 2013).

"The Generosity of the Past" and "Molting" were reprinted in *Verse-Virtual*.

I am deeply grateful to the following individuals for their support, encouragement, and advice: Barbara Elovic, Adele Kenny, Dean Kostos, Richard Levine, Djelloul Marbrook, Martin Mitchell, Larissa Shmailo, Chandra Young, and my publisher, Diane Lockward.

About the Author

Michael T. Young is the author of two previous poetry collections, *The Beautiful Moment of Being Lost* (Poets Wear Prada, 2014) and *Transcriptions of Daylight* (Rattapallax Press, 2000). He is also the author of the chapbooks, *Living in the Counterpoint* (Finishing Line Press, 2013), winner of the Jean Pedrick Chapbook Award, and *Because the Wind Has Questions* (Somers Rocks Press, 1997). His work has been published in such journals as *Cimarron Review*, *The Cortland Review*, *Little Patuxent Review*, *Potomac Review*, and *Valparaiso Poetry Review*. He is a past recipient of a poetry fellowship from the New Jersey State Council on the Arts and has been featured on *Verse Daily*.

www.michaeltyoung.com

www.ingramcontent.com/pod-product-compliance
Lightning Source LLC
Chambersburg PA
CBHW021446080526
44588CB00009B/710